I0812532

GOATs IN SPORTS

HOCKEY GOATs

KENNY ABDO

Fly!
An Imprint of Abdo Zoom
abdobooks.com

abdobooks.com

Published by Abdo Zoom, a division of ABDO, P.O. Box 398166, Minneapolis, Minnesota 55439. Copyright © 2025 by Abdo Consulting Group, Inc. International copyrights reserved in all countries. No part of this book may be reproduced in any form without written permission from the publisher. Fly!™ is a trademark and logo of Abdo Zoom.

Printed in the United States of America, North Mankato, Minnesota.
052024
092024

THIS BOOK CONTAINS RECYCLED MATERIALS

Photo Credits: Getty Images, Shutterstock
Production Contributors: Kenny Abdo, Jennie Forsberg, Grace Hansen
Design Contributors: Candice Keimig, Neil Klinepier

Library of Congress Control Number: 2023948516

Publisher's Cataloging-in-Publication Data

Names: Abdo, Kenny, author.
Title: Hockey GOATs / by Kenny Abdo
Description: Minneapolis, Minnesota : Abdo Zoom, 2025 | Series: GOATs in sports | Includes online resources and index.
Identifiers: ISBN 9781098285661 (lib. bdg.) | ISBN 9781098286361 (ebook) | ISBN 9781098286712 (Read-to-me eBook)
Subjects: LCSH: Hockey--Juvenile literature. | Hockey players--Juvenile literature. | Hockey--Records--Juvenile literature. | Professional athletes--Juvenile literature.
Classification: DDC 796.962--dc23

TABLE OF CONTENTS

Hockey GOATs 4

The Greats 8

Scoreboard 20

Glossary 22

Online Resources 23

Index 24

HOCKEY GOATS

From its beginning, hockey has been a **breakaway** sport thanks to the legendary players who have skated into the history books!

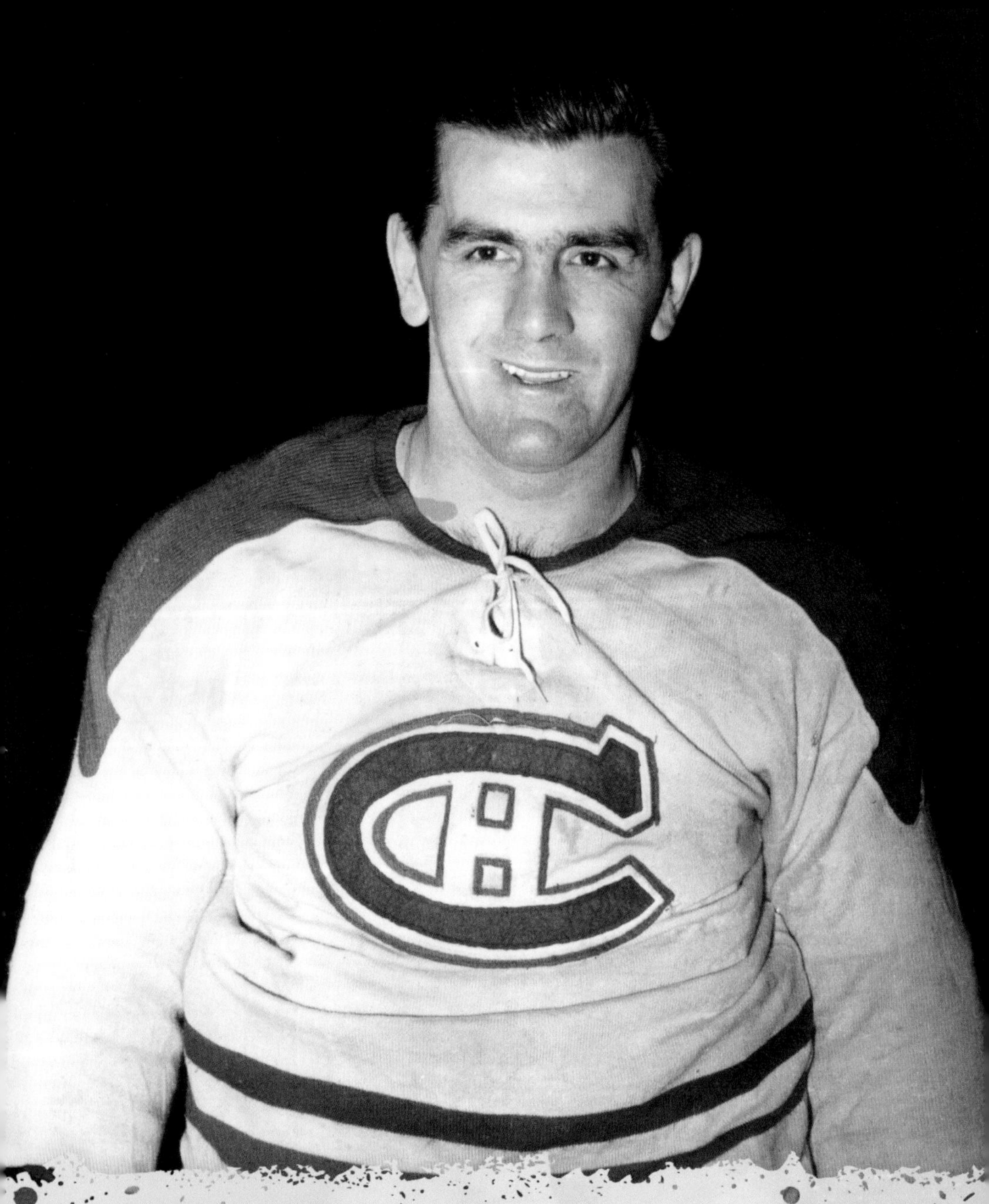

From Maurice Richard to Connor McDavid, hockey greats have brought the heat to this icy sport!

OILERS
CCM
delta
sonic

THE GREATS

Maurice Richard was one of the first icons of hockey. He played on eight **Stanley Cup championship** teams with the Montreal Canadiens. When Richard retired in 1960, he held 20 NHL records, including the most goals with 544.

Gordie Howe shined for 26 seasons in the NHL. His career began in 1946 with the Detroit Red Wings. At forward, he quickly became known for his ability to score. Howe played in more than 1,700 games spanning five decades!

Bobby Orr was a strong defenseman who could also assist and score. In 1970, he made the winning goal bringing the Bruins the **Stanley Cup**. It was the team's first in 29 years! Orr retired in 1979.

Wayne Gretzky was nicknamed the "Great one" for good reason. He ended the 1981–82 season with 92 goals, 120 assists, and 212 points in 80 games. He became the only player in NHL history to break the 200-point mark. Gretzky holds many records and held the **Stanley Cup** up four times.

Mario Lemieux **debuted** with the Penguins in 1984. He earned 100 points or more in each of his first six NHL seasons! Lemieux became the Penguins' team owner in 1999. He is the only man to have his name on the **Cup** both as a player and owner.

Patrick Roy was the goalie offensive players feared. Beginning his career with the Canadiens, he joined the Avalanche in 1996. Roy had 550 career wins and the most playoff wins by a goaltender by the time he retired.

Martin Brodeur spent most of his career as the Devils' goalie. He won four **Vezina Trophies** in five seasons. Brodeur broke Roy's record for total wins in 2009. His records of 125 **shutouts** and 691 wins have not been broken by a goalie since.

Alex Ovechkin **debuted** in the NHL in 2005. He clocked 106 points and was Rookie of the Year. In 2018, the Capitals won the **Stanley Cup**. That same year, Ovechkin became the fastest player in NHL history to take 5,000 shots on goal. His slap shot moved more than 100 mph (161 km/h)!

Sidney Crosby was **drafted** to the Penguins in 2005. He became the youngest captain to win the **Stanley Cup** at 21 years old! Crosby has since won two more Cups and two **Olympic** gold medals!

97
OILERS
CCM
24

Gliding toward hockey greatness, Connor McDavid has all the right moves. He was named Oilers' captain in 2016, becoming the youngest in NHL history at 19 years old! In 2022, McDavid became the sixth-fastest player in NHL history to reach 600 points.

SCOREBOARD

Fans of hockey watch for players to do the impossible on the ice. And these GOATs rank extra high in skills on the rink!

CARRIER
PANTHERS
AMERANT
FLORIDA
BAUER
CCM

GLOSSARY

breakaway – when a player has the puck and an open skating lane to the goal with no one in front of them.

championship – a game held to find a first-place winner.

debut – a first appearance.

draft – a yearly event in sports to when athletes are assigned to a certain team.

Olympic – of or relating to the Olympic Games. The Games are the biggest international athletic events held as separate winter and summer competitions.

shutout – in hockey, a game where the losing team does not score a point.

Stanley Cup – the elimination tournament played each year by qualifying teams in the NHL; the trophy awarded to the NHL playoff champion.

Vezina Trophy – an award given annually to the best NHL goaltender of the season.

ONLINE RESOURCES

Booklinks
NONFICTION NETWORK
FREE! ONLINE NONFICTION RESOURCES

To learn more about the GOATs in Hockey, please visit **abdobooklinks.com** or scan this QR code. These links are routinely monitored and updated to provide the most current information available.

INDEX

Avalanche 14
Brodeur, Martin 15
Bruins 11
Canadiens 8, 14
Capitals 16
Crosby, Sidney 17
Devils 15
Gretzky, Wayne 12
Howe, Gordie 10
Lemieux, Mario 13
McDavid, Connor 6, 19
Oilers 19
Olympics 17
Orr, Bobby 11
Ovechkin, Alex 16
Penguins 13, 17
Richard, Maurice 6, 8
Roy, Patrick 14, 15